WOOLBUDDIES

WOOLBUDDIES

20 IRRESISTIBLY SIMPLE NEEDLE FELTING PROJECTS

JACKIE HUANG

PHOTOGRAPHS BY ANTONIS ACHILLEOS

CHRONICLE BOOKS

SAN FRANCISCO

ACKNOWLEDGMENTS

I would like to thank all of the people who made this book possible:
Allison Weiner and Lisa Tauber at Chronicle Books, Lynn Bartsch,
my family, and, of course, everyone who has supported Woolbuddy—
without all of you, I wouldn't be here.

Text, how-to photographs, and illustrations copyright © 2013
by Jackie Huang.
Photographs copyright © 2013 by Antonis Achilleos.

Woolbuddy and all the characters, designs, and/or elements thereof
® and © by Woolbuddy. Used under authorization.

Library of Congress Cataloging-in-Publication Data available.

ISBN 978-1-4521-1440-8

Manufactured in China

Designed by Allison Weiner
Typeset by DC Typography

10 9 8 7 6 5 4 3 2 1

Chronicle Books
680 Second Street
San Francisco, California 94107
www.chroniclebooks.com

CONTENTS

INTRODUCTION

I have always had a love for the arts, and handmade crafts in particular. This passion drove me to study computer animation to foster my own creative skills, eventually landing me at Lucasfilm, where I worked as a 3-D story artist on the television series *Star Wars: The Clone Wars.*

When my first daughter was born, I searched for quality toys that were safe, durable, well designed, and that would instill in her an appreciation of handmade articles. What I found instead were cheap, plastic toys that were not meant to last. So I decided to put my creative background to good use and make toys myself.

I tried my hand at knitting and found it more challenging than expected. Sewing took too long, and I didn't have the patience to stick with it. Then I discovered needle felting and was immediately taken. With just a few basic tools and one material, I could see my designs take shape.

There really are no rules when it comes to this craft—you simply poke the wool until you are happy with the shape, and you can always add more wool on top to correct any mistakes. Felting is a lot like working with clay: you sculpt the fiber with your hands and a needle and turn it into fanciful shapes. But felting is much easier to do and, unlike clay, the final product is very kid-friendly. Perfect for my little daughter!

I started to illustrate and dream up the Woolbuddy characters, bringing them to life one by one with needle felting. At last, I was able to create the handcrafted stuffed animals that reflected the imaginative and magical world I wanted to share with my daughter. In just a few years, the Woolbuddy collection has grown to more than three hundred characters beloved by children and adults alike. The Woolbuddy world includes animals from the jungle, the farm, and the safari; sea creatures that frolic in the ocean; reptiles that lounge around the swamp; itty bitty critters that wander on land; and lovable monsters that live only in our imaginations.

In this book, you'll find instructions for making twenty of your very own buddies, from an adorably small guinea pig to a towering giraffe that stands over 1½ ft/46 cm tall. The sections are organized by complexity, although as you'll soon see, there's really very little skill needed to do this craft successfully while having fun along the way. Mainly, what matters is how much time you want to dedicate to making your buddy. Only have a short hour? Whip up Pointy the Starfish (page 47). Want to craft a three-dimensional statement piece? Get started on Hex the Octopus (page 99).

As you meet them, you'll see that no two Woolbuddies are identical. Each character has intricate detailing that only needle felting can create. The step-by-step instructions will guide you to make the buddies look as they are pictured, but I hope that you are inspired to explore your own imagination with this versatile craft. Swap out the wool colors for different ones, change the size of your buddy, or simply use the projects as a starting point for your own creations. That's the beauty of needle felting—you can easily change the size and appearance of any of your buddies' features while keeping pace with the instructions. Whether you're a first-time crafter or a felting pro, in no time at all you'll have a bevy of delightful creatures to enjoy and share.

—Jackie Huang

GETTING STARTED

⇌ WHAT IS NEEDLE FELTING? ⇌

Welcome to the wonderful world of Woolbuddies, which makes use of the popular fabric art process of shaping raw wool with special barbed felting needles. When the needle is pushed through loose wool, the needle's barbs catch and pull the fibers so they tangle and bind together to create a matted felt fabric. Using a single needle or a handheld tool with a cluster of felting needles, you can create any shape imaginable. What's more, with just a little practice, you can achieve fine and unique details. So grab some wool, a needle, and let's get started!

≥ TOOLS AND MATERIALS ≥

Needle felting requires only a few basic tools and materials, available at many craft stores and online. See Resources (page 112) for suggestions on where to purchase a variety of felting supplies. Following is a list of the felting tools and materials needed to complete the projects in this book.

FELTING NEEDLE

This needle is used exclusively for felting, as it is designed to push and interweave the wool fibers. Felting needles have a small lip at the top to make thrusting easier, though some needles attach to or are designed with a handle, which makes holding them even more comfortable. Needles are available in various sizes or gauges and commonly have a triangular blade. A star blade offers an extra blade edge, which can be useful for a faster finish if you are an advanced felter. A 36- or 38-gauge needle with a triangular blade works well for most felting work done with wool roving, which is what I recommend using for the projects in this book. A 38- or 40-gauge needle is best for finer fibers.

CAUTION: Please take great care when working with felting needles, which have tiny barbs along the bottom half and extremely sharp tips. Keep needles away from small children and pets and carefully supervise use by older children. Be sure to store needles in a safe place when not in use.

NEEDLE FELTING TOOL (OPTIONAL)

A handheld needle felting tool offers a comfortable grip and the option to work with multiple needles. Pen-style tools generally hold a few needles, while larger-capacity tools can hold as many as twenty needles at a time. While a tool like this isn't strictly necessary, the flexibility to work with a few needles at once will save you time when doing the less detailed work, such as creating a body base that requires a lot of needle poking. When you want to do more detailed work, simply remove the other needles and work with just one.

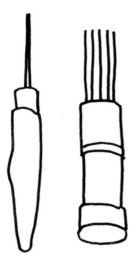

felting needle

barbs

— ouch!

MOLDS (OPTIONAL)

If you're new to needle felting or want to achieve a consistent look, you can use molds to guide you in making basic shapes. For example, you might use a star-shaped cookie cutter to make Pointy the Starfish (page 47). You can purchase premade molds specifically for needle felting. Just roll the wool, push it inside the mold, and gently poke to make your shape. Be careful not to poke at the mold itself, as this can break your needle.

THIMBLES (OPTIONAL)

Thimbles can be used to protect fingertips while felting and are great for those who are new to the craft. Since your dominant hand holds the needle, you really only need thimbles for the hand holding the wool. You can use thimbles on all fingers, or just the ones that may be most in the way of a sharp needle—your thumb, pointer, and middle fingers. Thimbles come in a range of colors and materials, including rubber, leather, and metal. Choose thimbles in the material of your choice that fit you comfortably.

WORK SURFACE

A felting pad or other soft work surface acts as a backstop, allowing the sharp point of the needle to pass through the wool and then safely catching the needle on the other end. Using a soft pad as your work surface will help you avoid breaking needles as well as accidentally poking your fingers, lap, or tabletop with a sharp needle.

You can use a variety of pads for needle felting, including a felting mat or a foam block. A brush pad–style felting mat has bristles to hold the wool in place while allowing the needle points to pass more easily through the fiber. The downside to a brush pad is that the bristles tend to pull at the fiber, making it fluffy again and requiring you to do some extra poking to smooth the shape. A foam block offers more protection if you prefer to felt on your lap rather than placing the felting pad over a firm surface, such as a tabletop. When using foam under your wool, avoid jabbing the needle repeatedly into the same spot as that can damage the pad.

You'll see that I've used a variety of surfaces when making my buddies; it's really up to you to decide which padding you prefer. While I tend to use a surface for forming only the finer detailing on my buddies (like ears and eyes), I recommend you start by always working on a felting pad or other soft surface until you get the hang of the process.

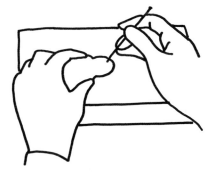

WOOL ROVING ·

Used for lots of different crafts, including spinning, wool roving is wool that has been combed, formed into a clump, then lightly twisted to hold the fibers together. Roving is sold by weight, rolled gently into a ball, and can be packaged separately or with a multitude of other colors. Look for wool that has a lofty, springy texture, without lumps. It should be loose and easy to pull apart, like thick cotton candy. The projects in this book call for wool roving such as Corriedale sheep's or other shorter fiber sheep's wool, which you can purchase by the ounce. Finer wools, such as alpaca and merino, are more challenging to work with because the fibers do not tangle together as easily, so you'll need to spend more time and effort poking them. Check the materials list included with each project to know how much roving you'll need in each color to make your Woolbuddy.

TECHNIQUES

The essential felting process is straightforward: Roll a piece of woolen fiber into the basic desired shape. Place the wool on your work surface and push the needle in and out of the fiber in a straight motion (i.e., needling) until it holds together and reaches the desired firmness. Here's a closer look at the process and some tips to make things easier.

NOTE: You can speed up the felting process by shaping the wool before you start poking. If you want a two-dimensional piece, flatten the wool with your hands to compress the fibers. For three-dimensional pieces, such as a body base or eyes, roll the wool into the desired shape and then get cracking with your needle. To learn how to make some of the basic shapes you'll use for Woolbuddies, see page 15.

WORKING WITH THE NEEDLE

Use your thumb and pointer finger to grasp the upper section of the needle. If you are working with a handled needle, you can hold it like a pen or a doorknob, depending on the design. Do not bend or twist the needle as you work. Felting needles are made of highly tempered steel, which means they are very sharp and brittle and can break easily.

Having rolled the wool piece into the basic shape, begin by making fairly deep needle jabs to reach the shape's center so the inner fibers as well as the surface fibers are felted. Turn the shape frequently as you poke so the fibers don't stick to the work surface.

WORKING WITH WOOL

Needle felting is a bit like sculpting with clay—you can make your project larger, add layers, and cover up mistakes by felting more wool onto your project. You can also poke to attach other felted pieces of the project to the main shape. For example, you will attach the Woolbuddies' limbs to the body. Felting wool is easier and holds better when the wool is fresh versus already felted. When felting the separate pieces, leave the roving loose on the end that will be attached to the main shape. This way the fluffy, unfelted fibers can be easily interwoven with the other felted piece. If you try to attach a fully felted wool piece to another fully felted wool piece, they may not attach seamlessly, since the fibers are already matted together.

NOTE: Felting can be a slow process—especially if you're working with only one needle—so find a comfortable place to work and be patient. (If you are working for several hours, remember to take an occasional stretch break.) Smaller projects with fewer intricate details will, of course, take less time than larger, more complex ones. A basic shape with a few details, such as Pointy the Starfish (page 47) or Shana the Penguin (page 25), could take anywhere from forty-five minutes to two hours, while Hex the Octopus (page 99) or Jimmy the Giraffe (page 87) could take a few days.

BASIC SHAPES

As you start to make shapes, you'll see just how easy it is to work with felt. You can sculpt it into any shape you like or combine many small parts to build your creatures. Here are some of the basic shapes that you'll use in almost all the projects. To practice, use as little or as much wool as you'd like. Refer back to these pages anytime you need a refresher.

MAKING A BASIC BODY SHAPE

1 Take a small handful of wool and begin to form an egg shape.

2 Use your hands to further roll the wool tightly to make the base for the body shape. By compressing the fibers together, the needle can pass through more of the shape at once (instead of just poking at air), thereby speeding up the felting process.

3 Place the wool piece on a felting mat, foam block, or other soft surface. Poke your needle repeatedly into the wool until it becomes the desired tube or egg shape that you'll use for most of the Woolbuddy body shapes.

4 If you want to form a roundish ball, position the shape on its end and poke at the top to push the tall side down.

5 Continue needling the wool until the shape is evenly round. Take care not to overwork. You're done when the fibers are interlocked, the body has a bit of give to it, and you're satisfied with the shape.

MAKING THE EYES

1 Take a scrap of white wool for an eye shape and start rolling.

2 Keep rolling the wool until it's a very firm ball shape.

3 Like so!

4 Place the ball on a felting mat, foam block, or other soft surface and needle it to lock in the shape.

5 For the pupil, take a pinch of black wool and roll it into a tiny ball. (You can add the pupil before or after attaching the eye shape to your woolbuddy.)

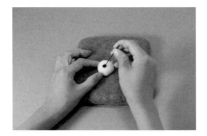

6 Use your needle to poke the dot into place on the eye shape. I usually put the pupil in the center of the eye, but feel free to play around with the location to change the expression. You can wrap a few strands of dark-colored wool around the eyes to add shadowing.

MAKING A FLAT SHAPE

1 Roll the wool tightly.

2 Fold it into your desired shape.

3 Put the wool on a felting mat, foam block, or other soft surface and poke repeatedly until it becomes flat.

4 Continue needling the wool to shape the corners as desired.

MAKING A CLEAN LINE BETWEEN TWO COLORS

1 To make a smooth, clean line between two colors, take the amount needed of the color you're adding on and fold it over to form a straight, even line.

2 Place the wool wherever this color should meet the base color and gently poke along the fold to set into place. Zeke the Rabbit (page 21) is an easy project for practicing.

SIMPLE WOOLBUDDIES

ZEKE

≋ THE RABBIT ≋

Everyone knows how much rabbits love their carrots, and Zeke is no
exception! Here, you'll practice making basic shapes and adding color
detail. To finish, you'll create a sweet treat for your rabbit friend to
nibble as he hops along the bunny trail in his trendsetting trousers.

Rabbit approximate finished size: 7½ in/19 cm tall by 6 in/15 cm wide
Carrot approximate finished size: 3½ in/9 cm tall by 1 in/2.5 cm wide

TOOLS AND MATERIALS

Felting needle
Felting mat or foam block

2 oz/55 g white or natural-colored
   wool (for the body base, ears,
   eyes, and arms)
Scraps of light brown wool
   (for the ears)
Small handful of brown wool
   (for the nose, eyes, and mouth)

Scraps of black wool (for the eyes)
0.5 oz/15 g blue wool (for the trousers)
Scraps of light blue wool (for the
   polka dots)
Small handful of orange wool
   (for the carrot)
Scraps of green wool (for the
   carrot stem)

MAKING THE RABBIT'S BODY

1 Take one-half of the white wool and roll it tightly into a thick egg shape.

2 Poke with the felting needle until the body is about 3 in/7.5 cm wide.

MAKING THE EARS AND FACE

3 Roll a small handful of white wool into a tube and poke it until firm, leaving the roving loose at the bottom end. Repeat for the other ear.

4 Put a pinch of light brown wool on the inner section of each ear and poke into place to secure.

5 Poke at the fluffy base to attach the ear to the body. Repeat for the other ear.

6 Set aside scraps of brown wool for the eyes and mouth. For the nose, roll the rest of the brown wool into an oval. Place it in the center about two-thirds of the way up the body and poke it into place.

7 Using scraps of white and black wool, make the eyes (see page 16). Poke at the base of the eyes to attach them just above the nose. Outline each eye with a strand of brown wool to create shadows.

8 For the mouth, roll a thin strand of brown wool and poke an upside-down T into place below the nose.

FINISHING THE BODY

9 Stretch and wrap the blue wool around the bottom of the rabbit's body, folding the top over and poking along the fold to make a clean line.

10 Roll pinches of light blue wool and attach to the trousers in a polka-dot pattern.

11 Divide the remaining white wool in half and roll each piece into a tube. Attach one arm to the side so it rests against the body. Partially attach the second arm, leaving the crook of the arm unattached to allow room for the carrot.

MAKING THE CARROT

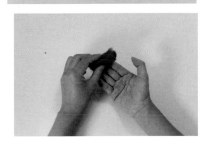

12 Roll the orange wool into a tube shape.

13 Place the orange tube in the unattached crook of the arm and poke to form a carrot shape. Needle at the base to attach the carrot and arm to the body.

14 Attach a scrap or two of green wool to the end of the carrot for the stem to finish.

SHANA
THE PENGUIN

What penguin doesn't love to waddle around and dive into icy waters? But Shana is a very special penguin: she was the first character introduced into the Woolbuddy world! In this project, you will practice applying color accents to your creature's basic shape in smooth, straight lines.

Approximate finished size: 4 in/10 cm tall by 3½ in/9 cm wide

TOOLS AND MATERIALS

Felting needle

1 oz/30 g white wool (for the body base, face, and eyes)

0.4 oz/10 g gray wool (for the body)
0.4 oz/10 g black wool (for the head, face, and eyes)
Scrap of yellow wool (for the beak)

MAKING THE BODY

1 Take three-quarters of the white wool and use your hands to roll it tightly into a ball.

2 Use the felting needle to poke the wool repeatedly to form a firm, oblong shape.

3 Stretch a layer of gray wool to fully cover the lower half of the body shape.

4 Attach the gray wool to the body by first poking the outer edges and working inward until the felt layer is smooth.

5 Take a small handful of black wool and attach to the upper half of the body, folding the top over and poking along the fold to make a clean line.

6 Continue poking to shape and attach the black wool so that it fully covers the remaining white shape and smoothly meets the gray section. The basic body will now be black on top and gray on the bottom.

MAKING THE FACE

7 Roll a small handful of white wool into an oval shape for the face.

8 Poke the white wool onto the front of the head, leaving a thick outline of black on all sides.

9 Attach a scrap of black wool where the head meets the face, continuing about halfway down the face.

10 Roll the yellow wool into a small ball and attach in the middle of the face to form the beak.

11 Using small scraps of white wool, make two eyes (see page 16). Poke at the base of the eyes to attach them on either side of the nose.

12 Roll two pinches of black wool into two tiny balls and poke into the center of each eye for pupils.

13 Outline each eye with a thin strand of black wool to create shadows.

14 A perfect start to a penguin family!

AMELIA
THE OWL

Her friends all assume Amelia is smart—and she is! With just a few easy steps, you can create your very own wise owl: just form a two-toned body, add some wings, and give Amelia her signature big blue eyes—or whatever color eyes you choose. A few more details and you're done!

Approximate finished size: 4 in/10 cm tall by 4 in/10 cm wide

TOOLS AND MATERIALS

Felting needle
Felting mat or foam block

1 oz/30 g white wool (for the
  body base)
0.3 oz/9 g dark brown wool
  (for the back and ears)
0.1 oz/3 g light brown wool
  (for the wings and belly)

0.1 oz/3 g light blue wool
  (for the eyes)
Pinches of black wool (for the eyes)
Scrap of yellow wool (for the beak)
A few strands of green wool
  (for the belly)

MAKING THE BODY AND WINGS

1 Take all of the white wool and use your hands to roll it into a ball. Then, use the felting needle to poke the wool repeatedly until it becomes an egg shape.

2 Set aside a scrap of the dark brown wool for the ears. Stretch the remaining dark brown wool to cover half of the body shape, folding it over to make a clean line, and attach by first poking the outer edges and working inward until the felt layer is smooth.

3 Set aside a scrap of the light brown wool for the belly. Divide the remainder in half and roll each piece into a ball. Layer over the seam of the dark brown and white wools on each side of the body, poke into a teardrop wing shape, and attach by needling.

MAKING THE EYES AND BEAK

4 Divide the light blue wool in half. Stretch one piece into an O-shape, place on the side of the face, and poke repeatedly to attach the eye to the head. Repeat to make and attach the other eye.

5 Continue needling each eye until it becomes smooth.

6 Take two pinches of the black wool and roll between your hands into two small, round balls. Poke into the center of each eye for pupils.

WOOLBUDDIES

30

7 Roll the yellow wool into a teardrop shape and poke into place directly beneath the two eyes.

8 To decorate your owl's belly, attach small green and brown dots in the pattern of your choice.

MAKING THE EARS

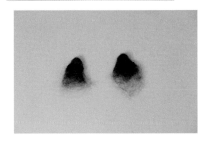  

9 Divide the reserved dark brown wool in half and place the pieces on a felting mat or other soft surface. Shape the pieces into two small triangles, leaving the roving lose on each bottom edge.

10 Attach each ear to the upper part of the head by poking at the fluffy base of the triangles.

11 What a hoot!

STANLEY
THE FROG

Give Stanley a kiss, won't you? He won't turn into a prince, but he's so cute that you might not be able to resist. Stanley is one of the simplest buddies to make: you'll just create a basic body, two imploring eyes, and then add any detailing you want. Best of all, he comes with his very own lily pad!

Approximate finished size: 4½ in/11 cm tall by 4 in/10 cm wide

TOOLS AND MATERIALS

Felting needle
Felting mat or foam block

1 oz/30 g white wool (for the
    body base and eyes)
0.3 oz/9 g green wool (for the
    body and lily pad)
A few strands of black wool
    (for the eyes)

Small handful of orange wool
    (for the arms and spots)
A few strands of brown wool
    (for the eyes)

For additional lily pad
Small handful of light green wool
    (optional)

MAKING THE BODY

1 Set aside two small handfuls of white wool for the eyes. Use your hands to roll the remaining white wool into a ball. Then, use the felting needle to poke the wool repeatedly until it becomes a round ball shape.

2 Reserve a handful of green wool to make the lily pad. Stretch a generous layer of green wool to cover half of the body shape, folding the top over to make a clean line.

3 Attach by first poking the outer edges and working inward until the felt layer is smooth.

MAKING THE EYES AND ARMS

4 Using the remaining white wool, create two eyes (see page 16), one slightly larger than the other. Poke at the base of the eyes to attach them side by side.

5 Roll two pinches of black wool into two tiny balls and poke into the center of each eye for pupils.

6 Reserve a few pinches of orange wool for the spots. To make an arm, take about one-quarter of the remaining orange wool and poke a small rectangle midway down the white side of the body. Attach three "fingers" by poking them directly onto the body: First space three dots a little distance away from the tip of the arm. Then add connector lines to link the fingers to the arm. Repeat for the other arm.

ADDING FINAL DETAILS

7 Wrap a few strands of brown wool under the eyes to create shadows.

8 Attach some small orange spots to the back for a final touch.

MAKING THE LILY PAD

9 On a felting mat or other soft surface, poke the remaining green wool into the shape of a flat, round pie with a slice missing.

10 Use the light green wool to make as many more lily pads as you like.

CECILY

≥ THE SEAL ≤

You may have seen Cecily (dressed in white) and her pals playing along the California coast. Make a new friend by creating this simple project that only uses three colors. With a project this easy and fun to do, you could even create a whole family!

Approximate finished size: 2½ in/6 cm tall by 6 in/15 cm long

TOOLS AND MATERIALS

Felting needle
Felting mat or foam block

1 oz/30 g white wool (for the body base, eyes, and flippers)

0.2 oz/6 g gray wool (for the mouth)
Small handful of black wool (for the nose, eyes, and flippers)

MAKING THE BODY

1 Take one-half of the white wool and use your hands to roll it into a ball. Then, use the felting needle to poke the wool repeatedly until it becomes an egg shape.

2 Take one-half of the remaining white wool and shape it into a rough triangle to make the tail. Poke to attach the bottom of the triangle to one end of the egg shape.

3 Continue needling the wool until the tail is smoothly fastened on and the basic body shape is extended into a flat, pointy end.

MAKING THE FACE

4 Roll the gray wool into a ball and attach it to the front of the body to form the mouth.

5 Roll a scrap of black wool into a small ball and attach it near the top of the gray area to create the nose.

6 Using scraps of white and black wool, make the eyes (see page 16). Poke at the base of the eyes to attach them above the nose.

MAKING THE FLIPPERS

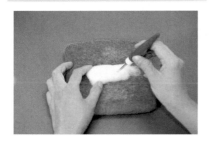

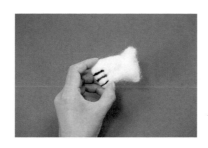

7 Divide the remaining white wool in half and place on a felting mat or other soft surface. Poke each section of wool into a soft, rectangular shape to create a flipper, leaving the roving loose on one short end.

8 Continue shaping the wool until your flippers look like this. Then, take a few strands of black wool and make stripes for claws on each flipper.

9 Poke at the fluffy base of the flippers to smoothly attach them on either side of the face below the nose area.

10 I'm ready for a swim!

MR. BINKS
≍ THE PIG ≍

Mr. Binks may be a little pig, but he's not afraid of the big bad wolf. In fact, they're friends! (Bill the Wolf is on page 59.) To make your own pig, you'll just need a basic body shape, eyes, ears, and a no-nonsense nose. Fashion his fancy striped pants in any colors you like and he's ready for a day on the farm and then some.

Approximate finished size: 4½ in/11 cm tall by 4½ in/11 cm wide

TOOLS AND MATERIALS

Felt needle
Foam block or felting mat

1 oz/30 g white wool (for the body base, pant stripes, eyes, and nose)
0.2 oz/6 g red wool (for the pants)

0.5 oz/15 g light pink wool (for the skin tone, arms, and ears)
Scrap of black wool (for the eyes and nose)

MAKING THE BODY

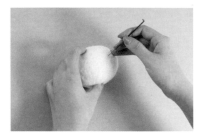

1 Take three-quarters of the white wool and roll it into a ball. Then, use the felting needle to poke the wool repeatedly until it becomes an egg shape.

2 Stretch the red wool to cover the lower half of the body. Attach by poking the outer edges and working inward until the felt layer is smooth.

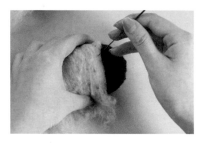

3 Stretch and wrap one-half of the pink wool around the upper half of the body and poke into place, folding the top over and poking along the fold to make a clean line.

4 Gently stretch a few strands of white wool, twisting to form a single strand. Lay the strand on the pants and poke into position.

5 Repeat step 4, laying the next stripe in the opposite direction. Continue adding stripes until you're satisfied.

MAKING THE ARMS

6 Set aside one-quarter of the remaining pink wool. Divide the remainder in half and roll each into a tube to create arms.

7 Starting just above the pant line, attach an arm to each side by poking directly into the body.

MAKING THE NOSE AND EYES

8 Take half of the remaining white wool and roll into a ball to create a nose.

9 Poke the nose into the bottom of the face, shaping it into an oval.

10 Using scraps of white and black wool, make the eyes (see page 16). Poke at the base of the eyes to attach them directly above the nose. Wrap a few strands of black wool around the eyes to create shadows. I made Mr. Binks's eyes different sizes to give him a quirkier look.

11 Use a few strands of black wool to add two parallel lines on the center of the nose for nostrils.

MAKING THE EARS

12 Equally divide the remaining pink wool. Shape into two flat triangles to create ears, leaving the roving loose on each bottom edge.

13 Poke at the fluffy base to attach each ear at the back top of the head to finish.

HANA

⇒ THE GUINEA PIG ⇐

This plucky guinea pig doesn't have to stay at home—she can come with you wherever you'd like! To create your own pocket size pal, you'll just need to make a few basic shapes and add some colorful details.

Approximate finished size: 2 in/5 cm tall by 3½ in/9 cm wide

TOOLS AND MATERIALS

Felting needle
Foam block or felting mat

1 oz/30 g white wool (for the body base and eyes)
Small handful of light brown wool (for the feet)

Small handful of dark brown wool (for the spots and ears)
Scrap of black wool (for the spots, nose, and eyes)

MAKING THE BODY

1 Set aside two scraps of the white wool for the eyes. Use your hands to roll the remaining white wool into a ball. Then, use the felting needle to poke the wool repeatedly until it becomes an egg shape.

2 Divide up the light brown wool to create four small balls for feet. Poke into place on the underside of the body shape.

3 Using dark brown and black wool, design your own guinea pig pattern by needling in different spot shapes and sizes. There's no wrong way to do it!

MAKING THE FACE AND EARS

4 For the nose, take a scrap of black wool and roll it into a ball. Poke into place on the front of the head.

5 Using scraps of white and black wool, make the eyes (see page 16). Poke at the base of the eyes to attach them offset above the nose. (I also added a few strands of dark brown under each eye to give Hana character.)

6 For the ears, take two scraps of dark brown wool and place them on a foam block or other soft surface. Shape the wool pieces into two loose semicircles, leaving the roving loose on the bottom edge. Poke at the fluffy base of the ears to attach on either side of the head to finish.

POINTY
THE STARFISH

Here's fun times five! Pointy the Starfish is an easy project to do—you'll learn to make a basic triangle shape and combine five of them to make your very own creature. If you're just starting out and want some help, you can use a large star-shaped cookie cutter as a guide for making the shape. Just be careful not to poke the metal or plastic—this will break your needle!

Approximate finished size: 6 in/15 cm tall by 6 in/15 cm wide

TOOLS AND MATERIALS

Felting needle
Felting mat or foam block

0.5 oz/15 g yellow wool (for the body base)

Scraps of brown wool (for the eyes)
Scraps of white wool (for the eyes)
Scraps of black wool (for the eyes)

MAKING THE BODY

1 Set aside a small handful of the yellow wool. Divide the remaining yellow wool into five equal sections. Place a piece of yellow wool on a felting mat or other soft surface and use the felting needle to shape the wool into a triangle, about 4 in/10 cm tall. Poke to flatten, leaving the roving loose on the shorter edge. Make four more triangles of the same size and thickness.

2 Configure the triangles in a star formation with the fluffy edges facing inward and slightly overlapping. Poke to attach the triangles to one another, adding a little more wool to the center of the star shape as needed.

3 Continue needling until the triangle pieces are smoothly attached.

MAKING THE EYES

4 To make the eye shadowing, lay scraps of brown wool in the center of the star and poke to attach, leaving a few wispy strands.

5 Using scraps of white and black wool, make the eyes (see page 16). Poke at the base of the eyes to attach them over the shadow piece.

MODERATE WOOLBUDDIES

EUNICE
≳ THE SHEEP ≲

Lucky for Eunice, she can needle felt all day long and never
run out of wool! So get ready, because you're about to connect
lots of tiny balls of wool to make a roly-poly sheep.

Approximate finished size: 4 in/10 cm tall by 5 in/12 cm wide

TOOLS AND MATERIALS

Felting needle
Foam block or felting mat

3 oz/85 g white wool (for the body
  base, wool balls, hooves, and eyes)

0.5 oz/15 g gray wool (for the
  wool balls)
1 oz/30 g black wool (for the legs,
  underside, head, eyes, and ears)

MAKING THE BODY ·

1 Take about one-sixth of the white wool and use your hands to roll it tightly into a thick egg shape. Then, use the felting needle to poke the wool repeatedly to firm up the body shape.

2 Take another small handful of white wool and roll it tightly into a round ball shape.

3 Lay the ball shape on a foam block or other soft surface and poke the wool repeatedly, rotating as you do so to form a smooth, firm ball, about 1 in/2.5 cm in diameter.

4 Following steps 2 and 3, use the white and gray wool to make 25 to 30 balls.

5 Poke repeatedly at the base of a felt ball to attach it to the body shape. Be sure it adheres firmly.

6 Repeat to attach the remaining felt balls to fully cover the top and sides of the body. Leave a space on the top of the body for the head and leave the underside completely uncovered. If your sheep has any bare spots, make and attach a few more wool balls.

MAKING THE LEGS

7 Roll a small handful of black wool to form a leg.

8 Gently work the wool into a tube shape, leaving the roving loose on one end.

9 Wrap a pinch of white wool around the opposite end of the leg to form the hooves and poke into place.

10 Repeat steps 8 and 9 to make three more legs the same size and shape, leaving the roving loose on one end and adding white wool to the bottom section to form the hooves.

11 Attach the fluffy ends of the legs to the body, placing a pair of legs at either end of the egg-shaped body.

12 Your sheep should look like this now.

13 Cover the underside area with some scraps of black wool.

14 Here's how it should look so far.

continued

MAKING THE HEAD

15 Roll a small handful of black wool into an oval shape. Poke the wool repeatedly until the head shape is firm.

16 Poke at the base of the head to attach it to the body.

17 Using scraps of white wool, make the eyes (see page 16). Poke at the base of the eyes to attach them side by side. Eunice has one eye that's slightly larger than the other, but feel free to make them equally sized.

18 Poke repeatedly at the base to attach each eye to the head. Roll two pinches of black wool into two tiny balls and poke into the center of each eye for pupils.

19 Take a scrap of black wool, lay it on a foam block or other soft surface, and poke into a flat oblong shape for an ear, leaving the roving loose at one short end. Repeat to make two ears.

20 Poke repeatedly at the fluffy base to attach an ear on either side where the head meets the body.

21 Baaa—you're done!

BILL

⪦ THE WOLF ⪧

Bill is a lean, lone, but super-friendly wolf! While he wants to be a ranger and protect the woods from danger, he's equally happy sacked out on your bookshelf. For this project, you'll layer color over an L-shaped body and then add features to give him a ferociously cute look.

Approximate finished size: 4½ in/11 cm tall by 2½ in/6 cm wide

TOOLS AND MATERIALS

Felting needle
Felting mat or foam block

1 oz/30 g white wool (for the body and head base, eyes, ears, tail, and paws)

0.25 oz/7 g dark gray wool (for the back and head, ears, tail, and arms)
Scraps of black wool (for the nose, eyes, and claws)

MAKING THE BODY

1 Take one-half of the white wool and roll it tightly into a tube. Then, use the felting needle to poke the wool repeatedly until it becomes smooth, but leave the roving loose on one end.

2 Take a small handful of the remaining white wool and make a smaller tube shape that will form the head, leaving the roving loose on one end.

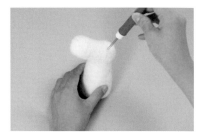

3 Place the smaller head shape per-pendicular to the body in an upside-down L position and poke at the base to smoothly join the two fluffy ends.

4 Take three-quarters of the dark gray wool, folding it over to make a clean line, and layer it evenly over the head and backside of the body. Attach by first pok-ing the outer edges and working inward until the felt layer is smooth.

MAKING THE FACE

5 Roll a couple of scraps of black wool to form the nose. Poke at the base to attach to the front of the head, needling until it becomes smooth. Using scraps of white wool, make the eyes (see page 16). Poke at the base of the eyes to attach them. Roll two pinches of black wool into two tiny balls and poke into the center of each eye for pupils. Then, needle a few strands of black around the eyes to create shadows.

6 Place scraps of dark gray wool on a felting mat or other soft surface and shape the pieces into two triangles, leaving the roving loose on each bottom edge. Poke a pinch of white wool into the center of each ear.

7 Poke at the fluffy base to attach each ear at the top back of the head.

MAKING THE TAIL AND ARMS

8 Take a few strands of dark gray wool and create a flat, long shape for the tail. Leave the roving loose on one end and wrap a pinch of white wool around the other end for the tip. Poke the white wool to adhere.

9 Attach the fluffy end of the tail to the lower back by poking repeatedly at the base.

10 For the arms, repeat step 8 by rolling two shorter lengths of dark gray wool into tubes and adding a pinch of white on the ends for paws. Poke the arms into place on either side of the body. Then, take a few short strands of black wool and poke them onto the white paws for claws to finish.

HENRY
⇒ THE FOX ⇐

Despite his adorably rugged style, this fox might be more writerly than woodsy. He has more than a few tall tales to go with the long tail you'll make up for him. The fox is a cousin to Dusty the Dog (page 67) and Bill the Wolf (page 59), as similar needle felting techniques are used to create all three. Let your imagination run wild to further customize these critters or invent entirely different ones!

Approximate finished size: 4½ in/11 cm tall by 2½ in/6 cm wide

TOOLS AND MATERIALS

Felting needle
Foam block or felting mat

1 oz/30 g white wool (for the body and head base, ears, tail, and paws)

Scraps of black wool (for the nose and eyes)
0.25 oz/7 g orange wool (for the back and head, ears, tail, and arms)

MAKING THE BODY

1 Take one-half of the white wool and roll it tightly into a tube. Use the felting needle to poke the wool repeatedly until it becomes smooth, leaving the roving loose on one end. Then, take a small handful of the white wool and make a smaller tube shape, leaving the roving loose on one end. Place the smaller head shape perpendicular to the body in an upside-down L position and poke at the base to join the fluffy ends.

2 Roll a couple of scraps of black wool tightly to form the nose. Poke at the base to attach the nose at the front of the head. Continue needling the nose until it becomes round and smooth.

3 Take three-quarters of the orange wool, folding it over to make a clean line, and layer it evenly, starting from the top of the nose, over the head, and down the back side of the body. Poke the outer edges first and work inward until the felt layer is smooth.

MAKING THE EARS AND EYES

4 Place scraps of orange wool on a foam block or other soft surface and shape the pieces into two triangles, leaving the roving loose on each bottom edge. Poke a pinch of white wool into the center of each ear.

5 Poke at the fluffy base to attach each ear at the top back of the head.

6 Using scraps of white wool, make the eyes (see page 16). Poke at the base of the eyes to attach them. Roll two pinches of black wool into two tiny balls and poke into the center of each eye for pupils. Needle a few more strands of black wool under the eyes to create shadows.

MAKING THE TAIL

7 Take a small handful of orange wool and create a flat, long shape for the tail, leaving the roving loose on one end.

8 Wrap a thin layer of white wool around the tip of the tail and poke to adhere.

9 Attach the fluffy end of the tail to the lower back by poking repeatedly at the base.

MAKING THE ARMS

10 Equally divide the remaining orange wool for the arms. Create two small tube shapes and add a pinch of white on the ends for paws.

11 Poke the arms into place on either side of the body to finish.

DUSTY

⇒ THE DOG ⇐

You can make your own best friend (and a friend for him, too!).
Here, you'll create and attach floppy ears and a thin tail, plus you'll
use different colors to create detailing.

Approximate finished size: 5 in/12 cm tall by 2 in/5 cm wide

TOOLS AND MATERIALS

Felting needle
Foam block or felting mat

1 oz/30 g white wool (for the body
  and head base, arms, eyes, and tail)
Scraps of black wool (for the nose,
  eyes, and back)

0.5 oz/15 g light brown wool
  (for the face, back of head, and back)
Handful of dark brown wool (for the
  tail and ears)

MAKING THE BODY

1 Take one-half of the white wool and roll it tightly into a tube. Then, use the felting needle to poke the wool repeatedly until it becomes smooth, but leave the roving loose on one end.

2 Use half of the remaining white wool to make a smaller tube shape, leaving the roving loose on one end.

3 Place the smaller head shape perpendicular to the body in an upside-down L position and poke at the base to smoothly join the two fluffy ends.

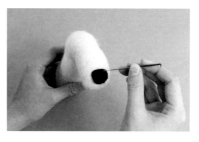

4 Roll a couple scraps of black wool tightly and poke at the base to attach the nose at the front of the head, needling the nose until it becomes smooth.

5 Take a small handful of white wool and roll into a tube shape for an arm. Attach to the side of the body and repeat for the other arm.

6 Take a small handful of light brown wool and stretch a layer over one side of the face, extending around the back of the head to the other side. Attach by first poking the outer edges and working inward until the felt layer is smooth.

7 Using light brown and black wool, create a design on your dog's back: it can be thick stripes of each color, spots, or you name it!

MAKING THE EARS AND EYES

8 Equally divide the dark brown wool into three parts. Using a foam block or other soft surface, create a flat, teardrop shape from one part for an ear, leaving the roving loose on the short end. Repeat for the second ear.

9 Poke at the base of the ear shape to smoothly attach a floppy ear to each side of the head.

10 Using scraps of white wool, make the eyes (see page 16). Poke at the base of the eyes to attach them to either side of the face, leaving a light brown border around each. Roll two pinches of black wool into two tiny balls and poke into the center of each eye for pupils. Then, needle a few strands of black around the eyes to create shadows.

MAKING THE TAIL

11 Using the remaining dark brown wool, create a long, flat shape for the tail. Leave the roving loose on one end and wrap a thin layer of white wool around the other end for the tip. Poke the white wool to adhere.

12 Attach the fluffy end of the tail to the dog's bottom by poking repeatedly at the base, and you're done!

ELLIE

⇒ THE ELEPHANT ⇐

Who needs fingers when you have a handy trunk and a pair of toothsome tusks? Crafting your very own elephant friend will let you try your hand at making some new and unique shapes. Weighing in at just over 4 ounces, Ellie (shown on the left) is the sweetest of elephants and cute to boot!

Approximate finished size: 6 in/15 cm tall by 4 in/10 cm long

TOOLS AND MATERIALS

Felting needle
Felting mat or foam block

4 oz/115 g light gray wool (for the body base, legs, head, trunk, and tusks)

0.5 oz/15 g white wool (for the trunk [optional], tusks, and eyes)
0.5 oz/15 g dark gray wool (for the ears and eyes)
Scraps of black wool (for the eyes)

MAKING THE BODY

1 Roll one-half of the light gray wool tightly into a ball. Use the felting needle to poke the wool repeatedly until it becomes a smooth, round shape.

2 Use scraps of light gray wool to create four small balls for legs. Poke into place on the underside of the body shape. Continue to needle the legs until they are even in length and flat on the bottom.

3 Your four legs should look like this. Try standing the elephant upright. If it's too wobbly, make sure the legs are all the same length and completely flat on the bottom. Add more wool if necessary to even out the leg lengths.

MAKING THE HEAD AND TRUNK

4 Set aside a couple of scraps of light gray wool to cover the ends of the tusks. Take the remaining light gray wool and make a tube shape for the head and trunk that's about 9 in/23 cm long and slightly thicker at one end. Poke repeatedly until the shape becomes smooth, leaving the roving loose at the thick end.

5 Poke at the fluffy base of the head shape to attach it to the body.

6 Poke the trunk so it nestles against the body. Now you have your basic elephant shape! If you'd like to decorate the trunk, take a small handful of white wool, wrap it around the bottom of the trunk and poke into place.

MAKING THE TUSKS, EARS AND FACE ···

7 Set aside a couple of scraps of white wool for the eyes. Divide the remaining white wool in half and gently roll each half into a cone shape for the tusks. Poke the wool repeatedly to firm and smooth each shape, making one end pointy and leaving the roving loose on the thicker end.

8 Poke at the fluffy base of each tusk to attach on either side of the trunk.

9 Here's how your elephant should look so far.

10 Add a scrap of light gray wool over the end of each tusk where it meets the body to cover the connective area.

11 To make the ears, divide the dark gray wool in half. Lay each half on the felting mat or other soft surface and poke into flat, rounded shapes, leaving the roving loose on each bottom edge.

12 To attach the ears, poke at the fluffy base to attach the ears to the head. Place a scrap of dark gray wool above the trunk for eye shadowing on the face. Using scraps of white and black wool, make the eyes (see page 16). Poke at the base of the eyes to attach them to the dark grey shadowing.

STRIPE

= THE ZEBRA =

A zebra's stripes are like fingerprints: each one has its own special pattern!
Here, you'll make the adult zebra shown on the right. Get creative in
this fun project by making your own pattern—add swirls, circles, or
any other shapes you can dream up.

Approximate finished size: 6 in/15 cm tall by 3½ in/9 cm wide

TOOLS AND MATERIALS

Felting needle
Felting mat or foam block

3 oz/85 g white wool (for the body
and head base, legs, mane,
eyes, and ears)

1 oz/30 g black or dark gray wool
(for the hooves, stripes, nose,
and eyes)
Scraps of light pink wool (for the
nose and ears)

MAKING THE BODY AND LEGS ···

1 Take half of the white wool and roll it into a ball. Then, use the felting needle to poke the wool repeatedly until it becomes smooth.

2 Roll a small handful of white wool into a tube shape.

3 Leave the roving loose on one end, wrap a pinch of black wool around the other end and poke into place for the hoof.

4 Poke to attach the fluffy end of the leg to one end of the body. Repeat steps 2 and 3 to make three more legs the same size and shape, leaving the roving loose on one end and adding black wool to the bottom section to form the hooves.

5 Attach the remaining legs to the underside of the body and poke to flatten the black ends so your zebra can stand. If it's too wobbly, make sure the legs are all the same length and completely flat on the bottom. Add more wool if necessary to even out the leg lengths.

MAKING THE HEAD AND MANE

6 Take a small handful of white wool and roll a tube shape for the head, making one end thicker and rounder than the other. Poke the wool repeatedly until it becomes smooth, but leave the roving loose on what will be the underside of the head.

7 Wrap a thin layer of light pink wool around the thick end of the tube to form the nose, and poke into place.

8 Poke at the base to attach the fluffy end of the head to the body.

9 To make the mane, lay a small handful of white wool on a felting mat or other soft surface and poke into a thick triangle. Leaving the roving loose on the long bottom edge, continue shaping the mane piece into a wide, short triangular shape.

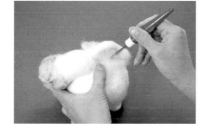

10 Position the mane lengthwise behind the head and poke repeatedly to attach the fluffy edge to the body.

11 Your zebra should look like this. If you'd like, take two scraps of black wool and create two vertical lines on the nose for nostrils.

continued

ADDING THE STRIPES

12 Roll several strands of black or dark gray wool together to create one long strand. Wrap the strand around the body and attach the stripe by poking the outer edges and working inward until the felt layer is smooth.

13 Continue making stripes and placing them in your desired pattern. Add some stripes around the legs if you like. There's no wrong way to do it!

MAKING THE EYES AND EARS

14 If desired, place a scrap of black wool above the nose for eye shadowing. Using scraps of white and black wool, make the eyes (see page 16). Poke at the base of the eyes to attach them side by side.

15 Divide the remaining white wool in half and felt two oval shapes for the ears, leaving some loose roving along one edge. Poke a pinch of light pink wool into the center of each ear shape. Fold each ear in half, then poke along the bottom of the fold to hold the crease in place.

16 Position an ear on either side of the head and poke at the fluffy base to attach to finish.

QUINT
THE SHARK

You might be surprised to learn that even though he's the smallest of the bunch, Quint the Shark is the principal of a school—the ocean's school, that is. To make the shark, you'll create several shapes, including triangles, to attach to the main body. To practice making triangles, whip up Pointy the Starfish on page 47.

Approximate finished size: 4 in/10 cm tall by 5 in/12 cm long

TOOLS AND MATERIALS

Felting needle
Foam block or felting mat

1.5 oz/40 g white wool (for the body base, eyes, and teeth)

1 oz/30 g blue wool (for the body, fins, and tail)
Scraps of black wool (for the eyes and teeth)

MAKING THE BODY

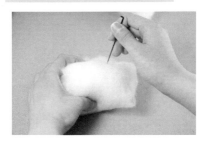

1 Take three-quarters of the white wool and roll it tightly into a thick egg shape.

2 Use the felting needle to poke the wool repeatedly to refine the shape, making it somewhat thicker at one end. Continue needling the basic body shape until it becomes smooth.

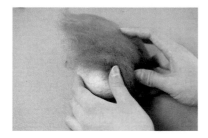

3 Stretch a layer of blue wool over the top half of the body shape.

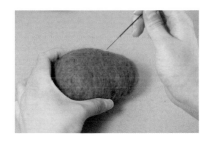

4 Attach by first poking the outer edges and working inward until the felt layer is smooth, making sure that the blue wool evenly covers the top portion of the body.

5 Keep the underside of the body white for the shark belly.

6 Take a small handful of blue wool and poke into place at the top front of the head to give a distinct shape to the shark's nose. Feel free to add more wool to make the shark even more three-dimensional.

continued

MAKING THE FINS AND TAIL

· ·

7 On a foam block or other soft surface, shape a small handful of blue wool into a triangle, about 2 in/5 cm tall. Poke to flatten, leaving the roving loose on the bottom edge. Make four more triangles of the same size and thickness for a total of five triangles.

8 To make the tail, lay the bottom points of two triangles together, slightly overlapping. Poke to attach the triangles to each other, adding a little more wool as needed. Leave the roving loose at the base.

9 Poke at the base to smoothly join the fluffy edge of the tail to the end of the body.

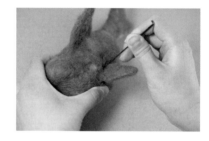

10 Position one triangle-shaped fin on the top of the shark's back and poke at the fluffy base to attach.

11 Attach the remaining two fins on either side of the body.

MAKING THE FACE

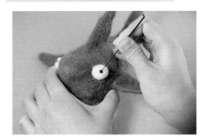  

12 Using scraps of white wool, make the eyes (see page 16). Poke at the base of the eyes to attach them to either side of the nose. Roll two pinches of black wool into two tiny balls and poke into the center of each eye for pupils.

13 Gently roll a scrap of white wool into a small cone shape. Poke the wool repeatedly to firm and smooth the tooth shape, making one end pointy and leaving the roving loose on the thicker end. Poke at the fluffy base of the tooth shape to attach above the white belly.

14 Make teeth in various sizes and attach across the mouth, pointing some up and some down. Poke scraps of black wool around the teeth to add contour. Then, needle a few strands of black around the eyes to create shadows to finish.

CHALLENGING WOOLBUDDIES

JIMMY

THE GIRAFFE

Jimmy is the tallest animal in the Woolbuddy kingdom, which means he needs a little extra help to stand on his own. In this project, you'll be wrapping your wool around wire to make Jimmy's legs more versatile—when you're done, he'll be able to stand, sit, or do kicks!

Approximate finished size: 20 in/50 cm tall by 5 in/12 cm wide

TOOLS AND MATERIALS

Craft scissors or wire cutter
Foam block or felting mat
Felting needle

48 in/122 cm length of 12-gauge craft wire
5 oz/140 g white wool (for the legs, body, neck, ears, and eyes)
Masking tape

0.3 oz/9 g black wool (for the hooves, nose, and eyes)
1.3 oz/40 g light brown wool (for the nose, ears, and spots)
1 oz/30 g dark brown wool (for the horns, spots, and eyes)
1 oz/30 g medium brown wool (for the spots)

MAKING THE LEGS

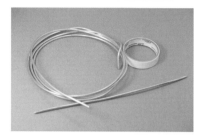

1 Use craft scissors to cut the wire into four equal lengths. Set aside a few handfuls of white wool and divide the remainder into four roughly equal amounts: two portions for the legs, one and a half for the body, and the rest for the neck and head.

2 Neatly wrap each length of wire with masking tape, which will make the otherwise slippery wire easier to work with.

3 Wrap each leg structure with several layers of white wool, starting at one end and working across, and leaving about 1 in/2.5 cm of wire exposed at the opposite end.

4 This is how each leg should look.

5 Poke the leg with the felting needle at an angle to smooth out the wool. Be careful not to poke directly on the wire, which may break the needle.

6 Turn the leg and continue needling on all sides until the leg is smooth, but leave the roving loose at the end where the wire pokes out.

7 Set aside a handful of black wool and divide the remainder into four equal amounts. Wrap one piece around the felted tip of the leg and poke to adhere.

8 The completed leg should look like this. Repeat steps 5 to 7 to make three more legs.

MAKING THE BODY

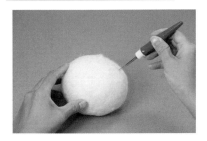

9 Tightly roll the portion of white wool reserved for the basic body shape. Then, use the felting needle to poke the wool repeatedly until it becomes smooth.

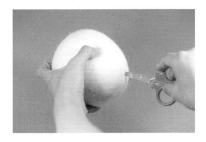

10 Use the scissors to make four tiny, equally spaced holes in the underside of the body for inserting the legs. The placement holes will ensure that the wire pieces are set well inside the body base, making the creature sturdier for standing.

11 Insert the wire end of a leg into a placement hole and poke at the fluffy base of the leg and body to attach. Take a small handful of white wool and wrap it around the leg to reinforce the leg's attachment to the body. Poke repeatedly to shape and smooth the newly connected sections.

12 Repeat step 11 to smoothly attach the other three legs, keeping them as close in relative length as you can.

13 For the neck and head, take another portion of white wool and roll it into a thick tube shape about 8 in/20 cm to 10 in/25 cm long. Poke repeatedly until it becomes smooth, leaving the roving loose on one end of the tube.

14 Poke at the base to attach the fluffy end of the neck to the body.

continued

MAKING THE HEAD

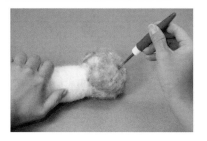

15 To make the nose, wrap a small handful of light brown wool around the end of the head and poke repeatedly to shape the surface into a round bulb.

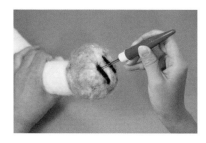

16 Needle a few strands of black wool to add two parallel lines on the center of the nose for nostrils.

17 Place a small handful of white wool on your work surface and poke into a flat, rounded shape for an ear, leaving some loose roving along one edge.

18 Poke a pinch of light brown wool into the center of the ear shape. Fold the ear in half, then poke along the bottom of the fold to hold the crease in place. Repeat to make the other ear.

19 Position an ear on either side of the head and poke at the fluffy base to attach.

20 For the horns, take two scraps of dark brown wool and create two small tube shapes.

21 Connect the horns to the top of the head between the ears.

ADDING COLOR DETAIL

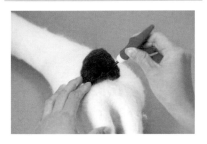

22 Use the three shades of brown wool to create a pattern of spots against the white background on the body. Poke the wool repeatedly until each spot is smooth.

23 Use the colors and shapes of your choice to make your giraffe unique.

24 Remember that the legs also need some color! I gave Jimmy some stripes.

MAKING THE FACE

25 Place a few scraps of dark brown wool just below where the eyes will go. Then, using scraps of white and black wool, make the eyes (see page 16). Poke at the base of the eyes to attach them above the shadow piece.

LILY

THE TIGER

Here's a pal to keep you company on your next safari. Lily has a big, flat face and a smaller body. You'll connect the two parts to make your own adorable tiger. This project offers the perfect opportunity to get creative with color. I used dark brown and dark green for Lily's stripes, but you could pick even brighter, more fanciful colors to make the tiger your own.

Approximate finished size: 7 in/18 cm tall by 7 in/18 cm wide

TOOLS AND MATERIALS

Felting needle
Felting mat or foam block

4 oz/115 g white wool (for the face and body base, cheeks, inner ears, eyes, and tail)
2 oz/55 g light green wool (for the face, nose, and body)

0.5 oz/15 g brown wool (for the nose, stripes, and ears)
Small handful of dark green wool (for the stripes)
Scraps of black wool (for the eyes and whisker dots)

MAKING THE HEAD

1 Take one-half of the white wool and roll it tightly into a thick cookie shape to form the face base. Then, use the felting needle to poke the wool repeatedly.

2 Take about half of the light green wool and stretch it in a thin layer over the front and around the sides of the face base.

3 Attach by first poking the outer edges and working inward until the felt layer is smooth and evenly covers the whole front of the face.

MAKING THE NOSE AND CHEEKS

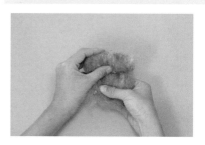

4 Take a small handful of the light green wool and roll it tightly into a tube shape for the nose.

5 Position the nose shape facing downward in the center of the face and poke repeatedly to attach.

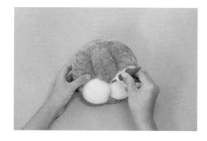

6 Take a small handful of white wool, roll it tightly into a small ball, and poke it under one side of the nose to form the first cheek. Make a second cheek shape and poke into place on the opposite side of the nose. Continue needling the cheeks until they are evenly round and smoothly attached.

7 Roll a scrap of brown wool into a ball and attach it to the end of the nose. Poke repeatedly to form into a triangular shape.

MAKING THE STRIPES

8 Take a small scrap of dark green wool and roll into a tube shape, narrowing one end to a point.

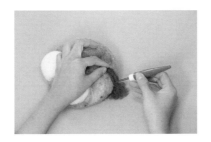

9 Attach the wool stripe to the side of the face with the pointy end facing inward.

10 Make more stripes in brown and dark green and attach to either side of the face in a pattern of your choice.

MAKING THE EARS

11 Take a small handful of brown wool and rub it in one hand to make an oval shape.

12 Place the wool on a felting mat or other soft surface. Poke it flat, keeping the oval shape and leaving a bit of the roving loose on a short end of the oval.

13 This is the basic shape of the ear.

14 Take a scrap of white wool, place it in the center of the outer ear shape, and poke into place to create the inner part of the ear.

15 Repeat steps 11 through 14 to make the other ear.

16 Poke at the fluffy base to attach an ear on either side at the top of the head.

continued

MAKING THE EYES

17 Using scraps of white wool, make the eyes (see page 16). Poke at the base of the eyes to attach them.

18 Needle a few strands of black wool around each eye to create shadowing.

19 Roll two pinches of black wool into two tiny balls and poke into the center of each eye for pupils.

MAKING THE BODY

20 Set aside a small handful of white wool for the tail. Roll the remainder tightly into a large oval for the body base.

21 Poke the wool repeatedly to firm up the body shape.

22 Use the remaining light green wool to cover the body base, leaving the covering loose on one short end.

23 Attach the fluffy end of the body base to the underside of the head.

24 Poke the fluffy end of the body base to firmly attach to the head, shaping the light green wool as needed to cover any remaining white on the back of the head.

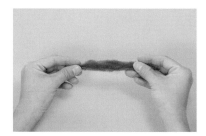

25 Use dark green and brown wool to create more stripe shapes.

26 Place colorful stripes on the tiger's back and around the body in a pattern of your choice.

27 Give your tiger as many stripes as you please!

MAKING THE TAIL AND WHISKER DOTS

28 To form the tail, take the remaining small handful of white wool and roll it into a thick cylindrical shape

29 On a soft surface, repeatedly poke the wool to shape the tail, leaving the roving loose on one end.

30 Take a few strands of brown wool and attach them on the tail to create stripes.

31 Attach the fluffy end of the tail to the bottom of the body by poking at a downward angle.

32 Roll several pinches of black wool into tiny balls to decorate the tiger's cheeks with whisker dots, and poke on to attach and finish.

HEX

⇒ THE OCTOPUS ⇐

Even though Hex only has six tentacles, he's just as sharp as his eight-tentacled friends. This hero of the deep lost two tentacles in battle but still manages to capture everyone's attention. You can, of course, make your octopus with eight tentacles, but the design can look somewhat busy that way. Plus, if you only give your octopus six tentacles, you can make up your own backstory about what happened to the other two.

Approximate finished size: 7 in/18 cm tall by 34 in/86 cm wide

TOOLS AND MATERIALS

Felting needle
Felting mat or foam block
Craft scissors

5 oz/140 g dark blue wool
  (for the tentacles and head)
0.5 oz/15 g light blue wool
  (for the spots)

0.2 oz/6 g white wool (for the
  head base and eyes)
Scraps of dark green wool
  (for the eyes; optional)
Scraps of black wool (for the eyes
  and suction cups)
Two 12 in/30.5 cm by 12 in/30.5 cm
  sheets of light-colored felt fabric
  (for the suction cups)

MAKING THE TENTACLES

1 Set aside a handful of dark blue wool for the head. Divide the remaining dark blue wool into six strips. On a felting mat or other soft surface, poke a strip of wool into a flat shape about 3 in/7.5 cm wide and 20 in/50 cm long.

2 Repeat with the other five strips. Some can be longer, some can be shorter. Round the corners on one end of each strip and leave the roving loose on the other end.

3 Use scraps of light blue wool to decorate the tentacles with spots on one side, poking the wool repeatedly until the spots are smoothly attached.

MAKING THE HEAD

4 Set aside a small handful of white wool for the eyes. For the head, roll the remaining white wool into a round ball and poke the wool repeatedly until it becomes a firm shape.

5 Take the remaining dark blue wool and stretch it over the entire head shape. Poke into place, making sure to evenly cover the base shape.

6 Feel free to use some more light blue wool to add spots or another pattern to the octopus's head.

7 Arrange the tentacles in a star shape with the fluffy ends inward and slightly overlapping. Poke the wool to join the tentacles together. Then, place the head in the center and poke to attach.

8 Using the reserved white wool, make the eyes (see page 16). Poke at the base of the eyes to attach them. Needle some strands of dark green wool around each eye to create shadowing, if desired.

9 Roll two pinches of black wool into two tiny balls and poke into the center of each eye for pupils.

MAKING THE SUCTION CUPS

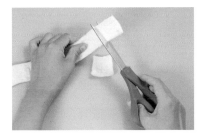

10 Cut the felt into long strips about 1 to 2 in/2.5 to 5 cm wide; make the felt strips narrower than the tentacles.

11 Cut the strips into square pieces.

12 Cut the squares into circles, making them different sizes. You'll need 60 to 100 circles, depending on the tentacles' sizes.

13 Attach a pinch of black wool in the center of each circle.

14 Poke the suction cups onto the underside of the tentacles to attach.

15 Continue until all the tentacles are decorated with suction cups to finish.

COGS

≡ THE ALLIGATOR ≡

Alligators don't have to be scary to behold or to make! By adding some big, bulging eyes and cute, crooked teeth, you can turn an alligator into a cuddly friend. In this project (the little guy on the right), you'll use your handy felting needle to make crease details—a cool way to add definition to the creatures you create. If the sculpting techniques used here seem a little daunting, try an easier version by making Quint the Shark on page 79. When you tackle the alligator, you'll already feel like a pro!

Approximate finished size: 3 in/7.5 cm tall by 6 in/15 cm long

TOOLS AND MATERIALS

Felting needle

1 oz/30 g white wool (for the body base, teeth, and eyes)
0.3 oz/9 g green wool (for the body)

Scraps of black wool (for the snout and eyes)
Scraps of brown wool (for the spots and eyes)

MAKING THE BODY

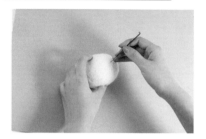

1 Take one-half of the white wool and roll it tightly into a thick egg shape. Then, use the felting needle to poke the wool repeatedly until the body shape becomes smooth.

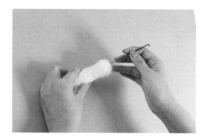

2 For the snout, roll a handful of white wool tightly into a tube shape. Poke the wool until smooth, but leave the roving loose on one end of the tube.

3 For the tail, make a slightly smaller tube, leaving one end fluffy.

4 Attach the fluffy ends of the snout and tail pieces to either end of the body by poking repeatedly at the base of the smaller shapes. Feel free to play with the shapes of the snout and tail by making them more bulbous or pointy.

5 Add a small handful of white wool to the top of the basic body shape for the head. You can further sculpt the creature and enhance the three-dimensional effect by adding more wool and poking it into the basic body shape. Puff up the belly or add some muscles—use your imagination!

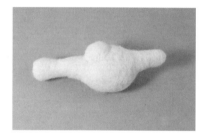

6 Here is the basic alligator body.

7 Set aside a small handful of green wool for the snout. Use the remaining green wool to stretch a color layer over the top half of the body shape.

8 Attach by first poking the outer edges and working inward until the felt layer is smooth, making sure that the green wool evenly covers the top portion of the body, snout, and tail. If you'd like, add small arms using the technique on page 34 for Stanley the Frog.

9 To create more detail and definition on the lower body, poke the same line repeatedly to form a visible crease running horizontally.

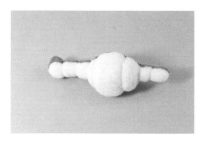

10 Make several creases across the body.

11 To add definition to the snout, divide the remaining green wool in half, form two balls, and attach on either side at the top end of the snout.

12 Add nostrils by rolling a couple of pinches of black wool into tiny balls and poking onto either side of the snout tip.

continued

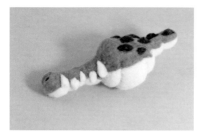

13 Use scraps of brown wool to create a pattern of spots on the back of the body—as few or many as you like. Make the spots lie smoothly or design them to look like bumpy scales. Poke the wool repeatedly until each spot is smoothly attached.

14 Don't forget: an alligator must have teeth! Gently roll a scrap of white wool into a small cone shape. Poke the wool repeatedly to firm and smooth the tooth shape, making one end pointy and leaving the roving loose on the thicker end. Poke at the fluffy base of the tooth shape to attach to the side of the mouth.

15 Make the teeth all different sizes and attach along both sides of the mouth, alternating pointing the teeth up or down.

16 Using scraps of white wool, make two eyes (see page 16). Poke at the base of the eyes to attach them right above the snout. Add black dots for pupils, and if you like, needle around the eyes with a couple of thin strands of brown wool for shadowing. Alternatively, place a few scraps of brown wool on the snout before attaching the eyes and then place the eyes over and slightly above the shadow piece as done for the giraffe on page 91.

17 See you later, gator!

TOBY

≥ THE BEAR ≥

Toby is the friendliest papa bear you'll ever meet—he's always ready
to wave hello! This project (the largest bear shown at top on page 108)
will take a bit of time, as you'll be covering a lot of the body base in
brown as well as making arms and legs with paw marks. But in the end,
you'll have a perfect partner for giving great big bear hugs.

Approximate finished size: 6 in/15 cm tall by 5 in/12 cm wide

TOOLS AND MATERIALS

Felting needle
Felting mat or foam block

1.5 oz/40 g white wool (for the body
base, limbs, mouth, tail, eyes, and
inner ears)

0.5 oz/15 g brown wool (for the limbs,
body, and head)
Several scraps of black wool (for the
nose, eyes, ears, paw marks, and
belly button)

MAKING THE BODY AND LIMBS ·······································

1 Take three-quarters of the white wool and roll it tightly into a ball. Then, use the felting needle to poke the wool repeatedly until it becomes a smooth egg shape.

2 Take a handful of the brown wool and separate into four equal amounts. Use one portion to make a tube shape about 3 in/7.5 cm long. Poke to smooth the shape, but leave the roving loose on one end of the limb.

3 Take a small handful of white wool and wrap around the felted tip of the arm shape to make a paw, folding the top over and poking along the fold to make a clean line. Repeat steps 2 and 3 to make the other arm and two slightly longer legs.

4 Pick two spots on the upper half of the body base and poke to attach the fluffy ends of the arms on either side. You may want to add some brown wool to the body base as you attach the arms. Do the same with the legs on the lower half of the base.

5 Here's how the attached arms and legs should look.

continued

MAKING THE HEAD AND BODY FUR

6 Take about one-fourth of the remaining brown wool and roll to create a round shape for the head. Poke to smooth the shape, but leave the roving loose on one long side of the shape. Then, poke to attach the fluffy part of the head to the top of the body. Continue needling the wool, adding brown wool as needed, until the head is smoothly attached and looks like an extension of the body.

7 Use a generous handful of white wool to make a big, flat felt ball for the mouth, first rolling the wool and then poking to flatten one side. Leave the flat side fluffy and attach the mouth to the front of the body, placing it a little below the crown of the head.

8 Roll a few scraps of black wool tightly to form a round nose shape. Poke at the base and attach the nose near the top of the mouth, needling until it becomes smooth.

9 Use the remaining brown wool to finish covering the body, leaving only the mouth, paws, and round belly exposed. To make a clean outline for the circular belly, fold over the brown wool to form one long strip and then wrap it around the body shape, outlining a circle of white.

10 Take a pinch of the white and roll it into a ball. Attach it to the bear's behind to make a small tail.

MAKING THE EYES AND EARS

11 Using scraps of white and black wool, make the eyes (see page 16). Poke at the base of the eyes to attach them to the far sides of the bear's head. Needle around the eyes with a couple of thin strands of black wool for shadowing.

12 To make the ears, grab a few scraps of black wool and two separate pinches of white wool. On a felting mat or other soft surface, use the black wool to make two circles. Put the white wool into the center of each circle and poke to smooth and flatten the ear shapes, leaving a bit of roving loose on the bottom of each circle.

13 Position the ears upright and connect the fluffy edge of each ear to the back portion of the head, in line with the eyes.

ADDING THE DETAILS

14 Set aside a few strands of black wool. To create paw marks, divide up the remaining black wool and use to add one large circle shape and three small dots to the white end of each arm and leg.

15 To give your bear a classic teddy bear finish, take the few strands of black wool and mark an X-shape for the belly button.

RESOURCES

You can find many of the tools and materials you need to get started with your felting projects at yarn stores, specialty craft stores, and online. To find yarn stores near you, visit www.knitmap.com, which has an extensive catalog of yarn stores around the globe. To order materials online, here are a few of my favorite suppliers.

WOOL

Harrisville Designs
Great selection of colorful yarns and fleece.
www.harrisville.com

Living Felt
Nice collection of wool, fleece, and felting tools.
www.livingfelt.com

Sincere Sheep
Sells naturally dyed wool.
sinceresheep.com

Woolbuddy
Visit to purchase wool, readymade Woolbuddies, and kits that include wool, felting needles, and instructions for many of the buddies not featured in this book.
woolbuddy.com

NEEDLES AND OTHER TOOLS

Clover
Sells a variety of needle felting tools, including the pen style that holds one to three needles.
www.clover-usa.com

FeltCrafts
Sells tools and needle felting machines.
www.feltcrafts.com

Jo-Ann Fabric and Craft Stores
Fabric and craft chain with large online shop.
www.joann.com